GW00320182

Caledonia Cooks

Caledonia Cooks

By Ipsita Y. Banerjee

Contributors:

Tapas & Shibani Banerjee
Zenaida Banerjee
Anjana Mazumdar
Debi Mukherjee
Sanghamitra Samadder
Pratap & Mala Som
Anu Vig

2017

Copyright © 2017 by Ipsita Y. Banerjee

All rights reserved. This book or any portion thereof may not
be reproduced or used in any manner what-soever without the
express written permission of the publisher except for the use
of brief quotations in a book review or scholarly journal.

Published by Golden Horseshoe Publishing Company
Hamilton, ON, Canada
www.goldenhorseshoepublishing.com

ISBN: 978-1-989372-70-8

Edited by Leah Fowler
Book Design by Ipsita Y. Banerjee

Dedication

This book is dedicated to the creative, courageous, loving spirits that shared their traditions, talents, dreams, and hopes with us and instilled culture, family, and community in our values.

And ... to the Cooks of Tomorrow.

Contents

Acknowledgements

My last visit to Toronto in September 2017 was a profound one. Looking back on the city that formed my earliest view on the world, it was humbling to learn to see and appreciate it from a visitor's lens. I returned to Toronto with a great deal of emotion – missing home, missing food, missing friends, and wondering if there was still a place for me there.

As I went from home to home, visiting each of my family members and learning about their cooking style as we worked together to create recipes that had been passed down through tradition, I learned a lot about each of them as unique individuals and what family meant to us. I realized as we reconnected that beyond our diverse and delicious food was a thickly woven fabric of emotions, memories, achievements, and hopes that kept us coming back to common gathering places to share, laugh, bond and grow with each other.

I would like to thank each of my family members for their unique contribution to this story about my beautiful family. I would also like to thank the following individuals for opening their homes and hearts to this project – sharing their experiences, feelings, wisdom, food, and love:

- Pratap & Mala Som, who shared "Malpuas" and "Chicken Curry with Vegetables and Beans"
- Sanghamitra 'Mini' Samadder and Anu Vig, who shared "Masoor Daal" and "Tandoori Chicken with Green Peppers"
- Tapas & Shibani Banerjee, who shared "Chicken Pakoras," "Aloo Tarkari and Luchee," "Okra with Posto," "Patol," "Fish Curry," "Malaicurry (Shrimp with Coconut Curry)" and "Goat Curry"
- Zenaida 'Zenie' & Jayanta Banerjee, who shared "Biko (Rice Cake)"
- Debi & Bhaskar Mukherjee, who shared "Mango Chutney"
- Anjana Mazumdar, who shared "Sandesh" and "Dai"
- Janis Som & Sanchita Jimenez, for wishing for this book to be created

I would like to thank my parents and sister for encouraging me to pursue my creative interests and to continuously learn and strive for more in life. I would also like to thank my nieces Amani & Anjali and my brother-in-law Eddie Jimenez, for their creative ideas and support. Finally, would like to thank my editor Leah Fowler and FabJobs, Skyler Burt from Digital Photography School, and Lulu Press for teaching me the technical skills I needed to create my first book!

Foreward

Dear People Reading This Book,

My name is Amani Jimenez. I am here to tell you why I helped with this book. I think I can help make this book better because I want to help people cook!

-Amani Jimenez, (Age 7)

Preface

Growing up in a busy, multicultural metropolis like Toronto, I often longed for the experiences "the other children" had. I wanted to know what it was like to vacation in chalets with grandparents, to swim in lakes at summer camp and to have teachers that could pronounce my name. It was not until I had some of those experiences as an adult that I was able to appreciate the unique life experiences I had growing up as an immigrant in Toronto. As newcomers in a new country, we created a new way of living together by bringing the best of our traditions together ... to make new ones.

"Caledonia Cooks" is more than a cookbook – it's an illustration of the beautiful people that raised and nurtured me and my community and a story of who we are as a family. Our meals may not have followed dietary guidelines, but you could taste the love wrapped around every bite, flowing through every dish, dancing in the air between laughter, stories, and music ....

As we grow, start families and move off to new places, and start exciting new life chapters, I wanted to create a place that we could always come back to and remember the journey that brought us together and the memories that filled our hearts. I hope we can to share these traditions with our children and create new traditions from the ones started in this book. I thank all the parents whose loving work is featured in this book. They gave wholly of their beings and shared the best of themselves with us all the time... smiling through their struggles as if they were not even there. They gave us the best gifts a generation could give: courage, love, support, inspiration, and talent.

I hope you enjoy reading and using "Caledonia Cooks" as much as I enjoyed researching and writing it.

-Ipsita Y. Banerjee, Author

Introduction

Caledonia Avenue was a neighbourhood filled with diversity. Immigrants to Canada often moved to communities like this in large cities like Toronto as it gave them a place to settle among others that were on a similar journey. My parents moved to Caledonia in the 1970s and there met other couples who would become their lifelong friends.

Migrating across oceans and continents often with little money and few keepsakes of 'home,' a shared culture was the strength that gave them familiarity in a foreign place. By continuing traditions like song, dance, theatre, folklore, decoration, cooking, and design, they created a community that celebrated its foundational traditions and shared these with others in their new place.

As children were born and the families grew, our bonds strengthened over time. Just as our parents did for their siblings and cousins, we supported each other through growing pains and found love, fun, and comfort in family events like parties, performances, and picnics. We loved finding any excuse to get together!

Religious ceremonies were numerous and gave us ways to learn about our values and ethics. The parents would spend hours cooking for the offerings to the Gods, which gave us lots of delicious food to enjoy afterward, as we socialized long into the night ....

By continuing cultural events like *bhai phota,* in which brothers and sisters honour each other, our parents taught us to honour and take care of each other - lessons that are evident today in the strength of our bonds across vast distances.

For as long as I can remember, I have always been surrounded by great food and people. Cooking - like fashion - gave us a chance to experiment with new ideas, share tips, and celebrate everything about us - our friendships, culture, values, and strengths. I hope you enjoy this journey into our culinary world!

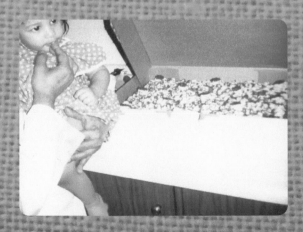

xo Ipsita

Starters &

Snacks

Chicken Pakoras

Makes 18-25 pieces

Ingredients

4 lb	Chicken legs, deboned and diced (not minced)
1 tsp	White vinegar
2 tbsp	Monosodium glutamate (MSG) (optional)
3	Onions (medium), peeled and diced small
3 tbsp	Garlic-ginger paste
1 whole branch	Fresh coriander leaves, chopped finely
2-3	Green chilies, finely chopped (optional)
4	Whole eggs
½ tsp	Soy sauce
½ tsp	Chili-garlic sauce
½ tsp	Honey or maple syrup
½ tsp	Ketchup
½ tsp	Mango sauce (if available)
1 lb	Tapioca starch
300g or ½ box	Corn Flakes
1 cup	Vegetable Oil

Procedure

- Rinse chicken in white vinegar and then rinse a few more times to clean and eliminate any odour. Then place chicken in a large bowl. Add MSG if desired, to tenderize meat.
- Add onions, then garlic-ginger paste, then coriander leaves and then green chilies. Combine until ingredients are evenly distributed.
- Add eggs, and then soy sauce, chili-garlic sauce, honey or maple syrup and mango sauce. Mix. Then add tapioca starch gradually to bind the entire mixture. Set aside.
- Now, place the wok on the stove on medium heat with enough vegetable oil to deep-fry the pakoras.
- Add corn flakes to the chicken mixture to add a crispy texture to the pakoras.
- Add 1 tbsp spoonful of the mixture to the hot oil and deep fry the pakoras. This will take about 5 minutes. Adjust the heat to prevent burning the pakoras.
- Place on in paper-towel lined bowl to absorb any excess oil. They are ready to serve.

Special Note: Green chilies are very spicy and may not be tolerated well by all your guests! Consider adding them to half of the batch to have *spicy* and *mild* options. Maggi Hot & Sweet sauce is a perfect complement to this appetizer and can be purchased in most ethic grocers.

Procedure

- Peel and cube 3-4 potatoes and then soak in water to prevent oxidization.
- In a pan on medium heat, melt *ghee* and add a pinch of onion seed. Add 1 tsp turmeric. Then add potatoes and fry until half-cooked.
- Add enough water to cover potatoes and reduce heat to simmer. Simmer for 10 minutes, or until potatoes are soft.
- Optional: add 2-3 fresh green chilies for extra spice and flavour.
- *Makes 10-12 servings.*

Aloo Tarkari

<u>Procedure</u>

- Sift 2-3 cups of all purpose flour into a bowl.
- Add a pinch of salt, a pinch of baking soda, and 2 tbsp of ghee. Mix.
- Gradually add warm water until a dough forms.
- Separate dough into 1-inch balls and roll out into round discs.
- Put enough oil in a work for deep frying and heat to medium.
- Gently release dough to the bottom of the wok, pressing lightly until it floats to the top and is golden. Remove before it browns. Serve hot. *Makes 30 pieces.*

Luchee

Malpua

Makes 20-25 pieces

Ingredients

6	Bananas (large), ripe and mashed
10	Cardamom (ground)
1 tbsp	Fennel seeds
¾ - 1 cup	All purpose flour
2 tbsp	Cream of wheat
¾ cup	Brown sugar
1 tsp	Baking powder
¼ - ½ cup	Milk
3 tbsp	Raisins
2-3 tbsp	Ghee (preferred), or butter or oil

Procedure

- Add ground cardamom, fennel seeds and cream of wheat to bananas and mix gently.
- Gradually add flour, combining by hand. Add just enough flour to form a gooey mixture. It should not be runny nor cake nor dough-like.
- Gently mix in brown sugar gradually, tasting to adjust to your sweetness preference.
- Mix in baking powder.
- Slowly add milk, blending gently and thoroughly with your hands until the mixture is smooth and free of lumps. Mixture should remain gooey. If it has become too runny, gradually add flour until the mixture is gooey and smooth. Taste and add extra sugar if needed.
- To test the hold of the mixture, take a spoonful and release it into the mixture. It should fall smoothly and gradually, maintaining a flexible, gooey form.
- Heat ghee on medium heat until melted and brownish (about 1 minute). Ensure it doesn't smoke to avoid changing the composition of the ghee.
- Spoon 1.5 tbsp of the mixture into the hot oil, forming small pancakes. Cook 2 minutes on each side, until golden brown and edges are brown and firm. Adjust heat as needed. No need to change oil between batches.
- Serve warm with tea, milk, or your favourite beverage. Enjoy!

Mains & Sides

Getting started...

Cooking can be a joyful experience if you have all of your ingredients in place and have prepared enough time and energy for the experience.

Most dishes include these common ingredients:

- Almonds
- Bori (Badi)
- Bay Leaves
- Cashews
- Cardamom
- Cinnamon
- Cloves
- Coriander
- Coriander Seeds
- Cumin Seeds
- Dried Chilies
- Fresh Chilies

- Chicken
- Coconut Milk
- Curry Powder
- Fish
- Flour
- Garam Masala
- Garlic
- Ginger
- Lemon or Lime
- Milk
- Mace
- Mustard Seeds

- Nutmeg
- Onions
- Onion Seeds
- Poppy Seeds
- Potatoes
- Raisins
- Salt
- Sugar
- Tandoori Spice
- Tomatoes
- Turmeric powder
- White Vinegar

Keep your kitchen stocked with these items so you can whip up your favourite dish whenever you want! Purchase small amounts of each to start from a bulk food store to keep costs low.

Tip: Make your own garam masala by combining 3 cloves, 3 cardamom and 3 cinnamon sticks in a blender. A little goes a long way!

Make or purchase your favourite sides (i.e., naan, paratha, roti, or rice) to accompany these delicous curries!

Masoor Daal

Makes 8-10 small servings

<u>Ingredients</u>

1 cup	Masoor Daal, whole
1	Onion (medium), chopped
1	Tomato (large), chopped
4 tbsp	Vegetable oil
3	Cinnamon sticks
Pinch	Cumin (ground)
½ tsp	Garlic-ginger paste
Pinch	Turmeric powder
Pinch	Curry powder
1 branch	Fresh coriander, washed and chopped
1	Green chili, whole (optional)
2-3	Curry leaves
½	Lime, juiced
	Salt
2 cups	Water

<u>P</u>rocedure

- Wash and boil masoor daal until very soft, then set aside.
- Heat oil over medium heat and brown cinnamon sticks and cumin.
- Then add onions and cook until browned. Then add tomatoes and brown.
- Add garlic-ginger paste, turmeric and curry powder. Stir.
- Add chopped coriander, green chili (if desired), curry leaves, lime juice and salt to taste.
- Add boiled daal to this mixture.
- Now add water and boil until mixture thickens. Add salt to taste.
- Serve with rice.

Tandoori Chicken
with Green Peppers

Makes 12 servings

Ingredients

5-6	Chicken breasts, cubed, washed, and dried
6 tbsp	Vegetable oil
4 tsp	Tandoori spice
1 tsp	Garlic-ginger paste
1 tsp	Salt
1 tbsp	Yoghurt
1	Onion (small), diced
1	Onion (medium), diced
1	Tomato (small), diced
2 tbsp	Water
Pinch	Turmeric powder
1	Whole chili (optional)
1-2	Green peppers, cut into chunks
1 branch	Fresh coriander

Procedure

- Prepare marinade by mixing 2 tbsp oil, 3 tsp tandoori spice, garlic-ginger paste, salt, small onion and yoghurt. Coat chicken in marinade and refrigerate for a few hours.
- Heat 4 tbsp oil over medium heat. Add onions and cook until browned.
- Add tomato and cook until browned. Then add marinated chicken.
- Stir continuously until cooked. Then add water, turmeric and 1 tsp tandoori spice. Reduce heat to low, cover and simmer for 5 mins.
- Add salt to taste (if required) and add whole chili for extra spice, if desired. Chicken and masala mixture should be dry.
- Mix in green peppers and coriander.
- Serve with naan, roti or rice.

Chili Chicken

Makes 2-10 servings

Ingredients

1	Chicken Breast
2-3 cups	Cold water
1 tbsp	White vinegar
½	Onion
5 cloves	Garlic, peeled
2 inch	Fresh ginger, peeled
	Vegetable oil
4-5	Green chilies, cut into small pieces
1-2 drops	Honey
1	Onion, sliced
	Tapioca starch
	Soya sauce

Procedure

- Blend ½ onion, garlic and fresh ginger until pureed. Set aside.
- Cut chicken into finger-sized pieces.
- Place chicken in a bowl with water and white vinegar to cleanse. Rinse 2-3 times.
- Add soya sauce and tapioca starch to chicken.
- Heat vegetable oil in a wok. Fry chicken until golden brown, then set aside.

- Add fresh oil to the wok. When the oil is hot, reduce heat to medium. Add the puree and stir until the mixture looks gray-brown.
- Add chicken to the mixture and continue to stir.
- Add 3 tbsp of soya sauce. As it cooks, add honey. Add additional tapioca starch as desired to thicken the sauce.

- Drench the sliced onion in tapioca starch.
- In a separate pan, fry onions until golden brown.
- On the serving dish, sprinkle sauteed onions and chopped green chilies over chicken.

Biryani

Makes 6-10 servings

Ingredients

1 ½ cup	Long grain Basmati rice
2-3	Cloves
1	Cardamom
1	Cinnamon Stick
1	Nutmeg (whole)
1	Mace (whole)
3 ½ cups	Water
10-12	Chicken thighs, skinned and trimmed
1 tbsp	White vinegar
3 tbsp	Ghee
2 tbsp	Ginger-garlic paste
1	Tomato, diced
2 tbsp	Biryani spice (any)
2 tbsp	Plain Yoghurt
1/4 cup	Cashews
1/4 cup	Raisins
	Milk with Saffron Crocus
	Rose or Keora/Kewra Water

Procedure

- Gently rinse rice in water and place on a cheesecloth to dry.
- Add cloves, cardamom, cinnamon, nutmeg, and mace in a tea bag.
- Bring half a pot of water to a boil. Add rice and tea bag and boil rice until the rice is half cooked. Drain excess water (called *akhani*) into a bowl and set it and the rice aside. If desired, add yellow food colouring and blend throughout.
- Place chicken in a bowl with cold water and vinegar. Rub until clean, then rinse in water.
- In a shallow pan, heat ghee over medium heat. Add onion and ginger-garlic paste. Stir for 3 minutes.
- Add chicken and fry until golden brown.
- Add tomatoes and Biryani spice. Stir until a shiny glaze forms over the mixture.
- Add 1-2 tsp water and yoghurt. Mix. Cover and cook on medium heat until the liquid has dried up. Set aside.
- Butter or grease a large pot and pan that has a lid. Over low-medium heat, add a layer of rice. Then add a layer of cashews, raisins, milk with saffron crocus, and a sprinkle of rose or Keora/Kewra water. Cover with another layer of rice.
- Add chicken mixture and cover with the final layer of rice. Sprinkle akhani water over all layers and cover with lid, ensuring no air leaks out.
- Reduce heat to low and let sit for 20-30 minutes.

Okra
with Posto

Makes 2-10 servings

Ingredients

4 tbsp	Poppy seeds, soaked in water for 6-7 hours
2 lb	Okra, washed, dried and trimmed
1-2	Onions (medium), sliced
3-4	Green Chilies
½ tsp	Turmeric powder
	Salt
4 tbsp	Vegetable oil

Procedure

- In a blender, mix poppy seeds with green chilies.
  To this, add turmeric powder and salt to taste.
- In a pan, heat oil over medium heat and then add onions and cook until golden brown. Add okras and fry until browned.
  Set fried vegetables aside.
- Reduce heat and now add the poppy seed mixture and stir slowly.
- Add fried vegetables to the poppy seed mixture and continue stirring until blended and cooked.
- Serve warm with rice, as a main or side dish.

Patol

(Pani Parwal)

Makes 5-6 servings

Ingredients

2lb	Patol (medium), peeled and sliced vertically
2 tbsp	Vegetable oil
Pinch	Onion seed
2 tbsp	Red mustard seeds
2 tbsp	Water
1 tsp	Turmeric powder
½ - 1 tsp	Salt
1	Coconut, shredded

Procedure

- Blend mustard seeds with water. Set aside.
- Wash patols and dry well.
- Heat oil in pan over medium heat. Add patols and fry until slightly brown. Set aside.
- Add 3 tbsp fresh oil. When the oil is hot, add onion seed.
- Add red mustard seed paste. Then add turmeric and salt.
- Add shredded coconut. Mix. Reduce heat to low-medium and cook slowly until all the water is absorbed. Add patols while cooking. This takes about 30-45 minutes.
- When all the water has been absorbed, the dish is ready.
- Serve with rice as a main or side dish.

Coconut Grinder

Chicken Curry
with Vegetables and Beans

Makes 6-8 servings

Ingredients

Rinse Solution:		
1 L	Water, warm	
3 tsp	White Vinegar	
2 tsp	Salt	

Marinade:		
1	Onion, chopped	
1 tsp	Salt	
½ tsp	Turmeric powder	
½ tsp	Ginger	
½ tsp	Cumin, ground	
2	Bay leaves	
1 inch	Fresh ginger, grated	
½	Lime (or ¼ Lemon)	
1 tbsp	Yoghurt	

3 lb	Chicken legs (thigh, drumstick)
3 cups	Leafy green vegetables (e.g., spinach, kale, rapini, etc.), washed, drained and chopped
1 cup	Beans, thawed if frozen, soaked if dried
2	Tomatoes (medium), chopped
6 cloves	Garlic, finely chopped
1 tbsp	Flour
1.5 inch	Fresh ginger
2 tbsp	Vegetable oil
2 tbsp	Whipping cream
½	Lime (or ¼ Lemon)
4	Potatoes, cut into 6 pieces each (optional)
4-5	Cardamom (whole)
6-7	Cloves
2 2-inch	Cinnamon sticks

Procedure

- Remove skin and fat from chicken, then soak rinse solution for 1-2 minutes. Drain solution and rinse again using fresh water.
- Prepare marinade and marinate chicken in this mixture. Refrigerate for 30-60 minutes or longer, and use within 4 hours.
- Heat vegetable oil on low-medium heat, being careful not to let the oil burn or smoke. Add garlic and cook until browned. Add flour and stir until browned. Add chicken. Cook for 5 minutes, covered.
- Add tomatoes and ginger, then turmeric and cumin. Add whipping cream, then the juice of ½ a lime or ¼ of a lemon. Stir. Add potatoes, if desired. Cover and reduce heat to low. Cook for 10 minutes. You should see some juices release.
- Add salt to taste. Uncover, and add vegetables and beans. Add cardamom, cloves, cinnamon, and chili powder and stir. Add ghee or butter and cover. Bring to boil and turn heat off. Let stand for 10 minutes to let flavours soak in.
- Serve with rice.

Malaicurry

Shrimp with Coconut Milk

Makes 7-8 servings

Ingredients

25-30	Jumbo Shrimp
	Water
1 ½ tsp	Salt
1 ½ tsp	Turmeric
1	Onion (medium)
5	Garlic cloves
1 inch	Fresh ginger
27 oz (2 cans)	Coconut milk
	Ghee
2	Bay leaves
3	White cardamom (whole)
3	Cinnamon sticks
½ tsp	Cumin
½ tsp	Sugar

Procedure

- Wash shrimp in warm water. Drain water and marinate shrimp in 1 tsp salt and 1 tsp turmeric.
- Heat oil in wok over medium heat. Fry shrimp until golden and set aside.
- Blend onion, garlic, and ginger into a smooth puree. Set aside.
- Now melt ghee over heat. Add bay leaves, cardamom, cinnamon sticks, and cloves.
  As they brown, add the pureed mixture.
- Add ½ tsp turmeric, ½ tsp cumin, salt, and sugar. Stir continuously on low-medium heat to prevent sticking.
- Add coconut milk and bring mixture to a boil.
- Now add shrimp and cook until the sauce thickens.
- The dish is now ready and can be served with rice.

Fish Curry

Makes 12 servings

<u>Ingredients</u>

3 1lb pieces	Salmon, washed, dried, and cut into ¼ lb pieces
½ tsp	Salt
½ tsp	Pepper
½ tsp	Turmeric powder
1 tbsp	Lemon juice
3-4 tbsp	Vegetable oil
¼ cup	Red poppy seeds, soaked in water overnight
¼ cup	Mustard seeds, soaked in water overnight
10-12	Green Chilies
2 tbsp	Plain Yoghurt
2 tbsp	Fresh Mustard Oil
Pinch	Onion seed
1 cup	Hot water

<u>Procedure</u>

- Create marinade for fish by combining salt, pepper, turmeric powder, and lemon. Drizzle over salmon pieces.
- Heat oil in a wok over medium heat. Fry fish one piece at a time until it releases a fragrant aroma. Remove fish from oil and place on a paper-lined dish to soak up excess oil. Then transfer fish to your serving dish.
- Rinse poppy seeds and mustard seeds. Add poppy seeds, mustard seeds, green chilies, and a few drops of water to a blender and blend until it becomes a smooth paste.
- Add yoghurt and mustard oil to the paste. Mix. Add salt to taste.
- In the same wok, add some fresh mustard oil. When the oil is hot, sprinkle in onion seed.
- Add mixture and stir over medium heat.
- When the mixture thickens, pour hot water over the mixture and bring to a boil.
- As the sauce boils, use a ladle to gently remove sauce and pour it over the fish. When all the fish has been coated with the sauce, let it sit to absorb the flavours.
- Serve with rice.

Goat Curry

Makes 16-20 servings

<u>Ingredients</u>

4 lb	Young Goat's Leg
1	Onion (small), finely diced
5-7 cloves	Garlic, peeled
4 inch	Fresh ginger
2-3 tsp	Turmeric powder
3 tsp	Coriander (ground)
1-2 tsp	Cumin (ground)
1 tbsp	Red chili powder or Kashmiri Mirch
½ tsp	Garam masala (home-made preferred)
2 tbsp	Ketchup
2 tbsp	Plain yoghurt
2 tbsp	Mustard oil
1	Onion (medium)
2-3	Bay leaves
1 tsp	Sugar
2-3	Potatoes (medium), skinned and cut into 4 pieces each

<u>Procedure</u>

- Trim fat from meat and wash well. Place in a pot. Bones are often left in for flavour.
- In a blender, blend ginger and garlic into a paste.
- Add ginger-garlic paste, the small diced onion, turmeric, coriander, cumin, red chili, garam masala, ketchup, yoghurt, and 4 tbsp mustard oil to the pot and mix until blended and the meat is covered in the mixture. Cover and refrigerate overnight.
- When you are ready to cook the meat, slice the medium onion and set aside.
- In a pot, heat mustard oil over medium heat. Add sugar. When sugar starts to caramelize, add bay leaves and onions. Cook onions until coated, but not brown or fried.
- Add marinated meat mixture to the pot with onions in slow and steady intervals. Stir regularly over 3-4 hours to prevent sticking to the pot and burning. Adjust heat between medium and high as needed.
- In the last 30 minutes of cooking, add potatoes.
- Continue to stir until it is ready. Enjoy with rice.

Mango Chutney

Makes 4-8 servings

<u>Ingredients</u>

2	Unripe green mangoes, skinned and cut into slices
½ tsp	Mustard seeds
2 tbsp	Vegetable oil
1-2 cups	Water
	Salt
	Sugar
¼ tsp	Cornstarch (optional)

Procedure

- Heat vegetable oil on medium heat and add mustard seeds. Add mango right away.
- Add sugar (or brown sugar) and salt to taste.
- Add 1-2 cups of water. Cover and reduce heat to low.
- Simmer for 15 minutes until mangoes are soft.
- Optional: add ¼ tsp cornstarch with water at the end to thicken, if needed or desired.

Variation

- Instead of mangoes, add an assortment of fruits (e.g., sour apples, apricots, pineapples, but avoid pears and bananas), cut into small pieces. Optional: add coriander leaves.
- For more spice, dry fry 8-10 ground coriander seeds and 8-10 ground cumin seeds. Sprinkle on top.

Mango chutney can be a wonderful companion to any meal.

Sweets

& Treats

Dai

Makes 8-10 servings

Ingredients

12 oz (1 can)	Carnation Evaporated Milk
4 oz	Plain Yoghurt (3.2%)
4 tbsp	Sugar

Procedure

- Blend Carnation Evaporated Milk, yogurt and sugar in a blender.
- Pour mixture in a oven-proof bowl.
- Put in the oven at 100 degree for an hour, at 150 degree for half an hour and at 200 degree for another half an hour.
- When dai has cooled, refrigerate to set or overnight.
- Serve chilled.

Sandesh

Makes 30 pieces

<u>Ingredients</u>

3 L	Homogenized Milk (3.25%)
¾ cup	White Vinegar
8 tbsp	Sugar
1 tsp	Vanilla Essence

<u>Procedure</u>

- Boil 2 and 3/4 litres of milk. When milk starts to rise add vinegar.
  Milk will change to solid called *chana*.
- Strain chana in water until water is gone.
- Boil the remaining 1/4 litre of milk until it thickens stirring occassionally to make *kheer*.
- In food processor, combine chana, kheer, and sugar, and process until the mixture turns into a dough.
- In a non-stick pan, add the dough and keep stirring until it is dry.
- When cold, food process again into dough.
- Roll dough into a small ball and place in the mould. Alternatively, place the entire dough into a square pot, flatten and cut into square pieces.

Biko (Rice Cake)

Makes 20 pieces

<u>Ingredients</u>

4 cups	4 cups uncooked extra-glutinous rice, soaked with 1 tsp salt for 7 hours or overnight
400 ml or 13.5 oz (1 can)	Coconut cream
2 ½ cup	Demerara brown sugar or molasses (no substitutes)
	Shredded coconut

<u>Procedure</u>

- Preheat oven at 350 degree.
- Leaving ½ inch of water above the rice, drain excess water.
- Boil rice with remaining water on stove, slowly adding coconut cream while stirring continuously to ensure the rice does not stick to the pan. The rice will get very thick and sticky. The rice will be ready when you see no more kernels; rice should pinch to a soft gel.
- Add brown sugar or molasses and stir. Rice should turn fully brown, leaving no kernel white.
- Transfer sticky rice mixture to a 13 x 9 inch baking pan.
- Bake at 350 for 60 minutes. It will be ready when the top and sides have hardened.
- Take the pan out of the oven and let the cake cool. When cool, place in the fridge to let it rest and firm up overnight (or longer, for better results). Cut into pieces.

<u>Toppings (optional)</u>

- Option 1. Shredded Coconut
- Option 2. Coconut Candy: Heat pan on medium heat. Drain liquid from coconut cream can and place coconut cream on hot pan. Melt and wait until the liquid starts to solidify, then remove from heat. The mixture will have little chunks of candy and syrup. Pour syrup on top of Biko and serve.

Payesh

Makes 15 servings

Ingredients

2L	Milk (2%, 3.25%, or Homo)
2-3 tbsp	Aromatic Basmati Rice, washed and dried
4	White cardamom (whole)
3	Bay leaves
1 small	Bark of Cinnamon
¼ cup	Golden raisins
¼ cup	Slivered almonds
4 tbsp	Sugar

Procedure

- Pour milk in a heavy-bottom pan and slowly boil over medium heat. Stir regulary and scrape bottom and sides with a spatula to prevent sticking. Adjust heat if milk starts to boil over.
- When the milk has reduced to half the volume, add rice, cardamom, bay leaves, cinnamon, raisins and almonds. Continue to stir until rice is cooked.
- Finally, add sugar and let it gradually melt in.
- Let stand and cool before serving. Flavours and consistency are often enhanced after 1-2 days of refrigeration.

Savour payesh as you celebrate milestones and honour traditions

New Beginnings

I end this book with the first solid food we eat as babies, Payesh. Payesh, a sweet, fragrant rice pudding is made to celebrate new babies, birthdays ... and anytime your mom wants to cheer you up! It is a reminder that every ending has a sweet and uplifting beginning in the renewing and forgiving cycle of life.

As our own fond childhood memories fade and new ones form with new friends, new babies, and new places, I hope you carry forward some of these traditions to share with your families and communities as our parents did years ago.

A few years ago, when I was struggling to find people and places that I connected with, I bought a cookbook and it changed my life. As I flipped though the pages racing to research all the new ingredients and words I was seeing, my eyes opened and I realized just how much there was to learn about the world around us, and also ... the world within us. As I journeyed from store to store looking for special ingredients like a scavenger hunt, it gave me a chance to become part of neighbourhoods, families, communities, and kindred spirits that I would never have encountered in my ordinary daily life. I hope this cookbook can do the same for you - helping you ask the questions and live the experiences that help you grow, challenge your assumptions, and build a deeper relationship with yourself and the fascinating world around you.

I learned many important lessons in the process of creating this cookbook ...

1) Cooking takes practice and patience.

Recipes, like our values, only give us a framework to start building on. As we experiment with new strategies and ideas, we have the opportunity to reinvent these traditional recipes with our own personality, preferences, and creative flair. Our tastebuds, asthetics, and company infuence how we make and enjoy the foods that we create. Always approach each recipe as an opportunity to learn about food, understand the cooking process, and explore your own ideas and preferences. Adopt the *art* of cooking by engaging your senses, planning enough time for the process, and opening your heart to the experience ... we have taken care of the *science* for you!

2) Where we end is never where we begin.

When I returned to visit my aunts and uncles, I was surprised that the recipes I had loved (and sometimes even craved!) had changed over time. The Cooks had experimented with new ingredients, different ideas, and found new venues and audiences to share their meals with, and the recipes evolved with the people they became. Flavours became more blended and refined, and the textures more smooth and natural.

3) Learn everything you can before you have the chance to forget.

After years of cooking on my own, I realized how many important steps and tips I had forgotten or missed in the time that had passed while I was *growing up*. There is no need to race to grow up! Take the time to be curious about everything happening around you. Practice with the experts and ask lots and lots of questions. Take notes, try ... and then try again! The journey is the goal, so soak up and seek out each experience and build on each step. Continue to learn about yourself and value every piece of it ... no matter what anyone says!

Thank you for joining me on this journey!

xo Ipsita

✷ *Meet the*

 *Shibani Banerjee*

 *Tapas Banerjee*

 *Jayanta Banerjee*

 *Zenie Banerjee*

 Anjana Mazumdar

Cooks *

Debi Mukherjee

Sanghamitra Samadder

Mala Som

Pratap Som

Anu Vig